Manifestes
7

Sep.
15

—HEAD
Publishing

Clémence Imbert
Why History Matters to Graphic Design

Why teach graphic design students the history of graphic design? This question might seem trivial. But nowadays, at some point in their training, graphic design students are bound to attend a lecture or course on the graphic design of previous decades or centuries, and it seems obvious that knowing about the work of at least some of the great graphic designers of the past is part of the culture they ought to acquire to join the professional ranks. And yet, as Steven Heller rather mischievously points out, why does a graphic designer need to know graphic design history any more than, say, a cop needs to know the history of the police or a butcher that of butchery (Heller, 2019, p. 5)?

This question is particularly pertinent in the context of art school, a realm fundamentally oriented towards the future of creativity. On the face of it, it would seem paradoxical to cultivate simultaneously the pursuit of the forms of the future and the study of old objects, outmoded forms and outdated techniques. How does historical knowledge inform present-day practice? How do students appropriate such knowledge? What creative skills do they develop through exposure to this subject matter?

But to begin with, how long has graphic design history been taught at art schools? It would seem sensible to start with a historical question—*since when?*—before seeking to shed light on the question of *why?* To understand the reasons for teaching graphic design history, we need to briefly review the history of training in graphic design.

Starting in the late 19th century, typography, a craft previously passed down for centuries from one generation to the next within printing shops, gradually came to be a discipline taught at more or less specialized schools and academies. Its standing evolved as the "graphic arts" became "graphic design", a multi-skilled discipline concerned with the form of texts and images, often both at once, and practiced mainly in the press, publishing, and advertising in the broadest sense.[1] Training in graphic design has diversified and expanded over time to include vocational and technical programs geared towards jobs in printing as well as curric-

1   On the history of teaching graphic design, see the essays compiled by Geoff Kaplan in *After the Bauhaus, Before the Internet: A History of Graphic Design Pedagogy* (New York, San Francisco: no place press, 2022), in particular Katherine McCoy, "Designing a Discipline", p.42–46, and Deborah Littlejohn, "Suspended Between Discipline & Profession: A History of Permanent Immaturity and Instability in the Graphic Design Field", p.48–59.

ula designed to develop not only practical skills, but also and above all proficiency in design and creativity, and increasingly rounded out by theoretical input—especially at schools of art and design. The latter now offer accredited—and in some cases selective—programs that attract students with varied profiles, and their pedagogical approach combines exercises designed to simulate the students' future professional work with workshops encouraging them to experiment and explore new, personal forms of expression.

There has been a great deal of discussion of specific features of graphic design training, its objectives and challenges, since the 1990s.[2] One reason for this is the sea change wrought by the advent of personal computers equipped with word-processing software, graphic design tools and compact printers. Now that anyone can claim to be a graphic designer and produce their own printed communications (posters, announcements, invitations, small-scale publications), what makes graphic designers special, except for the fact of having undergone training by and with their peers? It's no coincidence that it was precisely during this period of technological transition that the history

2   For example, "How We Learn What We Learn", a conference held in 1997 at the School of Visual Arts in New York, whose proceedings were published the following year under the title *The Education of a Graphic Designer* (1998), which has been reissued several times. See also Katherine McCoy, "Education and Professionalism or What's Wrong with Graphic Design Education?" (1997), in Teal Triggs and Leslie Atzmon (eds.), *The Graphic Design Reader,* London: Bloomsbury Visual Arts, 2019.

of graphic design took shape as a separate field of knowledge and became a more firmly established discipline in curricula, especially in the English-speaking world (Heller and Ballance, 2001).[3]

3   "During this formative period in the digital age, when new media is altering traditional notions of graphic design practice, it is even more important that designers have the grounding provided by historical knowledge." Steven Heller and Georgette Ballance (eds.), *Graphic Design History,* New York: Allworth Press, 2001, p. VIII.

For a long time before that, historical knowledge about graphic design had been imparted to students informally in workshop classes (Poynor, 2011). Students were familiarized with the names of the (predominantly male) "masters" and exemplary works of graphic design to guide them through certain exercises. Although Leon Friend, a teacher and the author of one of the first graphic design textbooks, devoted a significant amount of class time to teaching this subject at Abraham Lincoln High School in Brooklyn back in the 1930s (Friend, 1936), dedicated courses in graphic design history were not included in curricula until the 1970s. CalArts led the way by offering such a course in 1972, which was started up by Keith Godard and taken up the following year by Louis Danziger, who continued teaching it in various forms for twenty-five years there as well as at other American schools and universities (Heller and Ballance, 2001, p.329–336).

Like Friend before them, these two practitioners and historians focused their teaching on the outstanding figures in the discipline, who were associated with the main currents of modern art: Art Nouveau, Futurism, Dada, Bauhaus, etc. Keith Godard describes the primary pedagogical aims of his course as "to help students find role models that relate to their work" and "to realize [that] visual solutions are often repeated over generations, over time, especially with the advancing of production technology" (Godard, 2019, p. 23–24). The second objective clearly reflects an argument often adduced to explain the importance of graphic design history for aspiring practitioners: present-day graphic problems can often be solved by considering past solutions. Conversely, the American graphic designer Paul Rand, who taught at Yale, argued that knowing graphic design history should help avoid sterile repetition of what has already been done before.[4] Either way, these initial formulations suggest that the primary reason for teaching history to the next generation of graphic designers is its usefulness for creative projects. So it's no coincidence that this utilitarian argument is often advanced by teachers who are also practicing graphic designers.

4   "To shun history is to re-invent the wheel—with the probability of repeating what has already been done." Paul Rand, "Confusion and Chaos: The Seduction of Contemporary Graphic Design", *AIGA Journal of Graphic Design,* Vol. 10, No. 1, 1992 [www.paulrand.design/writing/articles/1992-confusion-and-chaos-the-seduction-of-contemporary-graphic-design.html].

As a result, the history of graphic design was deemed a subject for graphic designers only, to be written and taught only at schools of graphic design, as observed with some chagrin by British historian Rick Poynor (Poynor, 2011) in the early 2000s. He felt that this "design-history-is-for-designers point of view" had limited the development of knowledge and research in this discipline, relegating it to a mere background for practical training, with marginalized, institutionally fragile status—in other words, often with limited financial and human resources at its disposal. But things have changed over the past twenty years, in which graphic design history has gradually been taken up at universities, where it now forms a burgeoning field of research, and bolstered at art schools as well. Since the harmonization of higher education in the EU under the Bologna Process, students have been required to write a thesis based on their own research at the end of their course of studies, the form of which seldom differs from the models for university theses (Vandenbunder, 2016). Contemporary design practice has also developed some approaches to the investigation, construction and dissemination of knowledge that resemble academic research (Nova, 2021).

But despite all the vast areas of graphic design history that remain to be explored, history is not the field of inquiry preferred by "design researchers". As observed by the leaders of a recent research project on the history of Swiss graphic design:

> Design researchers have paid little attention to understanding design as a historical discipline that is produced by projects, methodologies, results, networks and discourses. This "historical amnesia" in design research strikingly corresponds to a lack of awareness of contemporary approaches in design history. (Scheuermann, in Fornari and Lzicar, 2016)

This harsh assessment may be tempered by citing a few counterexamples. The creation of new typefaces, now as ever, involves historical research, since documentation and in-depth familiarization with previous (in some cases, very old) typographic forms is indispensable to digitization projects and modern-day typeface "revivals". "Typography as we imagine it is always historical and, at the same time, always new," explain type designers André Baldinger and Philippe Millot. "What's new about it if the form is always historical? [...] The novelty lies in working on forms and counter-forms that have been tried and tested by history, on technological developments and new behaviors."[5]

As for editorial design, the established contemporary-art publishing sector shows a marked affinity for the idea of the archive. Witness the winners of the "most beautiful book" awards over the past twenty years, which have often gone to edi-

5   EnsadLab Type: André Baldinger and Philippe Millot, "Création de caractères typographiques: entre histoire et novation", in *Design graphique. Les Formes de l'histoire,* Paris: CNAP-B42, 2017, p.53. The EnsadLab Type research program ran from 2008 to 2014.

torial concepts that involve compiling images, texts and miscellaneous documents, halfway between catalogue and artist's book. In line with Hal Foster's theories on the "archival impulse" underlying contemporary art of the early 2000s, what we see here is an aspiration to historicize contemporary creation, to reject presentism (Foster, 2004).

Publications (whether print or digital) on graphic design history are also, in and of themselves, realms of creative research in which to reproduce historical material (images, archives, archival images and images of archives) both conscientiously and inventively. Cases in point include Coline Sunier and Charles Mazé's *Dossier Fernand Baudin* (2013) on the work of the eponymous Belgian type designer, whose handwriting served as the basis for the design of a new typeface, and Léo Favier's dissertation on Grapus, *Comment, tu ne connais pas Grapus? (What's that? You don't know Grapus?)*, published by Spector Books in 2014, which brings together in very Grapusian form various archival documents, photographs and interviews with the founders of this French graphic design collective (1971–1990). On the web, this kind of historical content also provides the material for experiments in screen reading under the guidance of design researchers, e.g. in the online magazine *Problemata*.[6] This "research platform focused on design history and critical studies" features an original interface, designed by the officeabc studio in collaboration with Thomas Bouville and

6   [www.problemata.org]

inspired by the forms of Olivetti typewriters and advertising (Ettore Sottsass and Giovanni Pintori). It constitutes a genuine form of "graphic research" combining ergonomic reading with interconnected content.

What is a reference?

Against this backdrop, graphic design history is taught in art schools nowadays in a wide variety of different forms and with all sorts of different objectives. The point here is not to explain what a graphic design history course should be or should do or produce, but to set forth and explore the arguments for its existence, content and pedagogical objectives.

It is widely held that history (whether of art, design or graphic design) is a fount of "references" for students to develop their personal culture and situate their work. Whether they are graphic designers or artists, students are expected to be able to back up their personal projects (particularly those submitted to obtain a degree) with references to the work of other creatives, and to situate and position themselves in relation to them. This reasoning combines the (very old) argument of influence or inspiration with a more modern demand: for students to come up with an unprecedented and original personal position, rather than repeating what others are doing or have already done. Stating their "references" is therefore presented first and foremost as an act of intellectual and artistic honesty, a way of demonstrating that they are aware that they are not alone and that they have not plagiarized.

But it's harder to describe how this little *musée imaginaire* filled by each student over the course of their training can make their practice more original, more personal, and enable them to stand "on the shoulders of giants". It's never a waste of time to remind students that the romantic myth of inspiration is precisely that, a myth, and that creativity does not come from faraway epiphanies, but, on the contrary, from material that's close at hand and intimately appropriated. The American psychologist G. F. Kneller observed in the 1960s that "one of the paradoxes of creativity is that, in order to think originally, we must familiarize ourselves with the ideas of others" (Kneller, 1965). But what are we to do with the work of others, especially those of centuries past? Or more to the point: How can we make something of it that is not mere name-dropping and goes beyond the stage of sifting —more or less in awe—through the inexhaustible stock of images to be found in books and on museum and library websites?

"Make connections to yourself and your work," advised Louis Danziger, one of the first to teach graphic design history at an art school (Heller and Ballance, 2001, p. 334). "The value of this course is in the connection you make. Using the course as a visual database is missing its true value." In a nutshell, the point of studying design history is to learn to "connect the dots", to "make connections" between graphic productions, between images, and compare them.[7] It's also a matter of creating a dialogue between different periods by finding contemporary echoes in what students see in class, learning to make out the historical layers underlying things in the present —and to be moved by them. As we shall see from the examples below, it is indeed the skills of a designer, a graphic designer, that come into play in this work of visually connecting the dots.

The first section of this essay will review some of the major historiographical debates through the prism of pedagogy: How does graphic design history relate to art history? What are we to make of the history of styles and major (often white male) figures? And, above all, how can students appropriate this knowledge, which sometimes seems to them so remote from their world and their concerns, and make it resonate with the present? The second part of the essay will describe the design skills that may be kindled by engaging with design history, in particular the exercise of the analytical eye, aesthetic decentering, the ability to navigate vast corpora of images and explore terrain hitherto uncharted by Wikipedia. The third part of this essay argues

7   These exercises in making connections are core elements of the pedagogical approach established by Emily McVarish at CalArts (Heller, 2021, p.207–236) and by Silvia Sfligiotti at the Istituto Superiore d'Arte d'Urbino in Italy (Sfligiotti, 2022).

that, far from being merely a field of expertise and a source of material for academic exercises, graphic design history is a discipline that can inspire next-generation graphic designers, hone their sensibilities and put their skills to the test.

1

WHICH HISTORY?

It's never been easier to learn about graphic design history than it is now, in the mid-2020s. Never before have there been so many books and documentary films about the subject and such easy access to reproductions of posters, books and magazines on the websites of public collections and online archives. This material is brought to life by the social media accounts of institutions and enthusiasts who regularly share their latest finds and curiosities: book and album covers, signs, painted advertisements and the like. A penchant for things "vintage" has boosted the popularity of the graphic productions of past decades. While it may kindle their curiosity, students often feel paralyzed by the sheer glut of images and information because their general knowledge of history is, in many cases, shaky; they have a hard time getting their bearings and wonder what to retain.

Furthermore, graphic design history only became a separate discipline some forty years ago. The 1983 "Coming of Age" Symposium at the Rochester Institute of Technology marked the birth of graphic design history as a recognized field of academic endeavor by bringing (mostly American) teachers and researchers together in upstate New York (Hodik and Remington, 1984). Its objectives, methods and connections to other disciplines have been ongoing subjects of debate ever since (de Smet and de Bondt, 2012). Generally speaking, its initial historiographical phase in the 1970s and '80s revolved around laying the groundwork for this field of study and identifying its major exponents and stylistic currents over the course of a great narrative timeline reaching all the way back to the first traces of human culture (Müller-Brockmann, 1971; Meggs, 1983). Beginning in the 1990s, the limitations of this approach were gradually brought to light by self-styled critical historians, who made the case for an approach to history divested of the formalist analysis of masterpieces and giving greater consideration to the political, social, ideological and technological contexts of graphic practices (Jobling and Crowley, 1996; Drucker and McVarish, 2009).

Another dimension of these historiographical debates was the lack of inclusivity in graphic design history, whose canonical narrative had long remained fixated on white male figures (Scotford, 1991). While general works on graphic design history often claim to cover a large number of different countries, they actually center on the West: continental Europe, England and the United States, with an occasional glance at the Cuban and Japanese schools of poster making. Now that research is increasingly illuminating women's and minorities' role in the history of graphic design and graphic productions in the Global South,[8] the narrative is opening up—which is particularly desirable in view of the fact that most graphic design students are female, and today's classes are far more culturally diverse than in the past.

However, while it's important to present these historiographical debates as an integral part of graphic design history, they're more than likely to add to the students' perplexity rather than helping them discover an immense realm and engage with the graphic forms and ideas of the previous century. Specifically, how can we meet their legitimate expectations of being introduced to beautiful images, figures they can identify with and key references in the "general culture" of their future profession? Which history—or histories—should they be taught? And how should we handle stylistic and authorial categories in the contemporary context?

8   See, for example, Bahia Shehab and Haytham Nawar's important study *A History of Arab Graphic Design* (Cairo: American University of Cairo Press, 2020). This dynamic is also observable on platforms like Futuress.org (created by designer Nina Paim in 2019), which is committed to decolonial and inclusive approaches, or BIPOC Design History (created by graphic designer Silas Munro in 2021), whose object is to rewrite design history from the viewpoint of Blacks, Indigenous and People of Color [bipocdesignhistory.com].

Recycling the graphic styles
of yesteryear

One of the major conceptual and aesthetic revolutions of the second half of the 20th century was born of a pedagogical experiment. *Learning from Las Vegas,* a report on a study trip undertaken by professors Robert Venturi, Denise Scott Brown and Steven Izenour with some of their graduate students at the Yale School of Art and Architecture, came out in 1972. The book points out the "contradictions and complexity" of urban planning in Las Vegas and the city's pervasive popular penchant for ostentatious decoration and pastiches of historical architectural styles. This "architectural unconscious", which ran counter to the rationalist and universalist principles informing architectural design on the East Coast at the time, shook modernist thought to its foundations.

Along with architecture and object design, graphic design was also shaken up by this challenge to its guiding precepts of clarity, legibility and universality, which it thought had been achieved in the minimalist style of Zurich graphic design, which was emulated all over the world. 1980s graphic design raises profound questions about legibility and, more to the point for our purposes, about the cyclical nature of graphic trends and the possibility of indulging in pastiches of past graphic styles (Heller and Chwast, 1988).[Fig. 1] Paula Scher's famous 1984 "copycat" poster for Swatch is a pastiche of a 1930s poster by Swiss designer Herbert Matter intended to draw tourists to the Swiss Alps. Louise Fili draws inspiration from Art Deco signs for her book covers, packaging and posters. Emigre, a digital type foundry and magazine based in Berkeley, California, and run by Zuzana Licko and Rudy VanderLans, was doing pioneering work in computer graphics and bitmap fonts, and was even being compared to Dadaism (Poynor, 2003). Against this backdrop, New York graphic designer Paul Rand wrote an article for the American Institute of Graphic Arts entitled "Confusion and Chaos", condemning the mix of genres within the mix of styles:

> Omnipresent, decorative letterspaced caps; visually annotated typography and revivalist caps and small caps; pseudo-Dada and Futurist collages; and whatever "special effects" a computer makes possible. These inspirational decorations are, apparently, convenient stand-ins for real ideas and genuine skills. [...] That these clichés are used repeatedly, irrespective of needs, is what defines trendiness. (Rand, 1992)

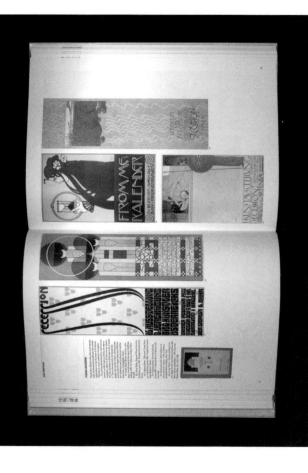

According to Rand, the history of styles should proceed in Darwinian fashion by selecting the best: "The historical process is (or should be) a process of distillation and not accumulation. In a certain sense it is related to natural selection —survival of the fittest." Symptomatic of modernism's faltering self-assurance, this view seems, from a present-day perspective, quite reductive. On the other hand, Paul Rand's indignation does point up the question of the conceptual validity of stylistic pastiche and quotation and the risk of reducing work on meaningful substance to the production of appearance without any substance.

What Rand failed to perceive, however, was that the historicist references of postmodern graphic design in the 1980s and '90s, far from being superficial, testified to a fundamental questioning of graphic design as an area of creative endeavor and of the means it employs as well as the status of its practitioners—giving rise at the same time to a theoretical leap forward and putting graphic design on the road to becoming a genuine discipline (Poynor, 2003). For there's no denying that graphic design ties into history and its own history in a powerful way: the forms of yesteryear often furnish the raw material for new creations. As graphic designer and editor Scott-Martin Kosofsky writes, "In graphic design, being interesting and alluring—and clear—is always the higher truth. It's what we're after. But it is also a field that, like architecture and fashion, makes use of its past in a remarkably full

[Fig. 1] Steven Heller and Seymour Chwast, *Graphic Style: From Victorian to Post-Modern,* 1988

way, often for entirely different purposes" (Heller, 2019, p.31). This is obviously the case in type design, which can never wipe the slate completely clean of the letterforms established in antiquity and the Middle Ages. But above all, because visual communication always depends on the addressees' familiarity with certain graphic forms, which construct the underlying system of connotations. How then can we help students master the possibilities of stylistic quotation in a way that goes beyond mere formal imitation?

In 1988, amid the prevailing mood of postmodernism, Martha Scotford carried out a project with her design students at North Carolina State University involving a "typographic translation" of Vladimir Mayakovsky's famous poetry collection *Dlia Golosa (For the Voice)* as interpreted typographically by El Lissitzky in 1923. Mayakovsky's text experiments with the limits of poetic language, integrating onomatopoeia and street language into an energetic orality. Its typography illustrates Lissitzky's ideas about the typography of the future (as set out in *"Topographie der Typographie"*, an article published in the avant-garde magazine *Merz* the same year). *For the Voice* was published in Berlin in the form of a small volume, printed in red and black, of 13 poems arranged on 13 double-pages, each of which can be readily accessed by means of a thumb-index system. Each double-page contains an "illustration" composed of typographical signs (letters, punctuation marks and geometric ornaments) on the left and a poem on the right, whose layout provides indications for reading it aloud.

By the time Scotford and her students began working on the book, Mayakovsky's poems had already undergone several translations from Russian into English, none of which retained the original Cyrillic forms. "This is the locus of the 'problem' for the translator and for the non-Russian reader of these poems, as designed in this book: how can both the literature and the art, which are so inextricably connected here, be translated and transposed into another language which is written with a different set of symbols" (Scotford, 1988, p. 200). With the help of a professor of Slavic literature and after in-depth documentary research on the original booklet's Constructivist context, printing techniques and visual poetry, the students developed the most convincing graphic equivalents possible to produce a translated facsimile edition.[Fig. 2] Scotford summed up the project's achievements and pedagogical contributions in the magazine *Visible Language*: "Pedagogically, this project served several goals: (1) a vehicle for learning more design and typographic history; (2) a way to appreciate the inventiveness of Lissitzky; (3) a contemporary twist on the methodology of copying the Masters" (*ibid.*, p. 220).

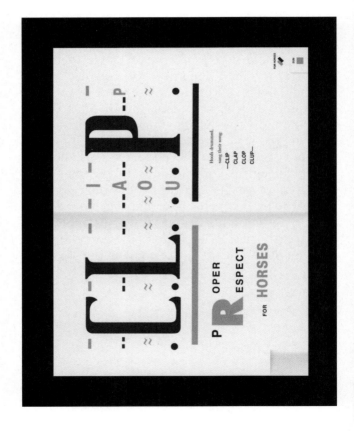

Why History Matters to Graphic Design

[Fig. 2] Vladimir Mayakovsky, El Lissitzky, *For the Voice* [1923], English translation: Peter France, typographical translation: Martha Scotford, Cambridge: MIT Press, British Library, 2000

Which history?

However, one of the first battles in the critical history of graphic design—and one in which Martha Scotford got involved very early on (Scotford, 1991)—concerned efforts to deconstruct the linear "portrait gallery" narrative with which the first historians of graphic design (Josef Müller-Brockmann, Philip B. Meggs, Richard Hollis) sought to establish the discipline and distinguish its (mostly male) leading exponents. Scotford points out not only its sexist and Western-centric biases, but also its pedagogically reductive nature: "For students new to the study of graphic design, a canon creates the impression that they need go no further; the best is known, the rest is not worth knowing. This is unfair, dangerous, and shortsighted" (Scotford, 1991).

For educational purposes, however, it's difficult to tell a story without characters. The biographical approach is obviously conducive to identification, which is one way of linking the present and the past. Louis Danziger observed that his students:

Develop a greater commitment to their work, which they now see as part of a continuum. They see themselves as part of something, perhaps the next contributors to this history. [...] Although I believe in the importance of contexts and historical imperatives, I think that, particularly in design history, the idiosyncratic personality is of prime importance! (Heller and Ballance, 2001, p.330)

His aim was to introduce students to the pioneers of graphic design from a perspective that valorizes individual personalities and anecdotes.

However, presenting graphic designers as autonomous creative individuals runs the risk of overlooking certain aspects that fundamentally distinguish graphic design from other forms of creation, especially the visual arts. Immersing oneself in the career of a major graphic designer should, above all, highlight not so much the stylistic coherence of a hypothetical "œuvre" as the versatility that characterizes this profession and its actors, who can be seen producing posters, magazine layouts, photographs and works of art, designing exhibitions, teaching and writing. By tracing an individual designer's career, students can follow the ever-changing technical constraints with which they had to come to terms, and which compelled them to reposition themselves ideologically and/or stylistically.

Over the past ten years, graphic designer and teacher David Reinfurt has been teaching a graphic design course in the Visual Arts department at

Princeton University. The course brings together students from a variety of different backgrounds, for some of whom this is their first contact with the discipline, and it combines theoretical input with practical exercises. In 2018, Reinfurt condensed the course into six 45-minute lectures, which were held over three days and subsequently formed the basis for a book (Reinfurt, 2020). Broken down into three themed parts ("Typography", "Gestalt" and "Interface"), which are covered in that order, one per semester, Reinfurt's "*New* Program for Graphic Design" introduces a number of canonical figures, including László Moholy-Nagy, György Kepes, Max Bill, Muriel Cooper, Bruno Munari and Susan Kare, presenting their personal and educational histories in detail as well as sketches and various stages of their work, photographs taken in their studios and excerpts from interviews. In short, it shows these graphic designers as individuals who are looking for solutions, not already in possession thereof. Reinfurt's pedagogical approach includes practical work designed to help students understand the overarching technical concerns in the history of graphic design. The class's first assignment is to compose a page on a traditional letterpress machine. A few weeks later, they are to put themselves in the shoes of a typesetter back in the days of phototypesetting and lay out a text in columns using a photocopier, glue and scissors. These practical exercises help them gain a greater appreciation for the inventiveness of the major designers covered in the syllabus by coming to grips with the technical constraints under which they were working.[Fig. 3]

The biographical approach also enables students to think about how we gain access to posterity. How is history written? Which projects, which practitioners, deserve to outlive their own day and age? It's always useful to drive home to students that the intrinsic merit of any given work plays a small role compared to the social construction of renown, the role of professional associations, networks and institutions. Hence the importance to many teachers of bringing to light neglected sides of history, especially the contributions of women, minorities and non-Western countries to the history of graphic design.

Briar Levit, a professor at Portland State University, has started up a collaborative database called "The People's Graphic Design Archive" and encouraged her students to use and enrich it.[9] This crowdsourced virtual archive is founded on the principle that "everyone should decide what is a part of graphic design's history". Anyone can upload their finds (finished projects, photographs, correspondence, oral histories, texts, etc., provided they were produced at least ten years ago). The archive includes fanzines and gay zines, militant pamphlets, luggage tags, album covers, even TV cartoons and title sequences. Students are asked to select an entry from the archive and write a brief history thereof (no more than 2,200 characters), which will then be posted on the university's Graphic Design Instagram account. In addition to providing a few elements of context, they should

9   [www.peoplesgdarchive.org]

These titles inevitably betray Muriel Cooper's deep investment in synthesizing design with an intimate knowledge of production. *File Under Architecture* was produced entirely with the IBM Selectric, where quick and immediate typeface changes were as simple as replacing the typographic ball. Margins were set in multiple typefaces as a running commentary. The book was printed on butcher's paper and bound in corrugated cardboard. The result [→] looks like the process that made it and reveals a deep engagement with and symbiotic relation between the design and production of the book.

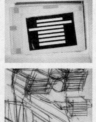

For *A Primer of Visual Literacy* [→] all typesetting again was produced on an IBM at the MIT Press. However, this time the result is not immediately recognizable as typewriting. The book was set in a crude proportionally spaced version of Univers, the sans serif typeface designed by Adrian Frutiger (who also designed the standard Courier letters).

Perhaps the most visible mark that Cooper left at the MIT Press was the design of the publisher's mark in 1964. In an early sketch for the logo, a shelf of books is clearly legible, viewed from an idealized axonometric projection. A row of seven books sit neatly next to each other with (conveniently) the fourth pulled up and the fifth pulled down. The result is an abstracted form of the abbreviation "MITP" or MIT Press. Flattening the mark to form a series of positive bars of equal width results in a clear barcode—as the products of mass production sit together in an orderly row, dematerialized into the pure information of a machine-readable graphic. This important piece of graphic design already contained

many of the concerns that Cooper would follow in the next 30 years probing the limits of mass production and exploring the impact of digital information [↗] [↘].

As a publisher's mark, the MIT Press logo is called a colophon. More generally, a colophon refers to the page of a book that details its production process—who typeset it, who printed it, when it was printed, what edition it is, library catalog references, etc. It is a convenient coincidence that Cooper's legacy at the Press is most clearly lodged in both of these colophons—on the spine in a highly formalized graphic and on the last page, where production details are tallied.

At MIT Press, there were yet some books with which Cooper would be personally and comprehensively involved as the designer. One prime example is *Bauhaus: Weimar, Dessau, Berlin, Chicago* by Hans Wingler published in 1969. Supported in part by an NEA grant and additional MIT Press funding, she would spend most of two years designing and producing the book. The "Bauhaus Bible," as it's widely known, contains the definitive collection of documents from the German art school through its multiple locations and bureaucratic arrangements. The book includes correspondence, descriptions of each workshop, budgets, and photographs documenting the species of the school. She described the subject matter of this book as a perfect fit, a coincidence of subject, designer, and situation. The book design was given enough time to happen in a comprehensive manner and the stunning result reflects it. Cooper described the fortunate synchrony of subject matter and design brief:

explain how the object in question relates to a current (political, aesthetic, technological) issue: "This is the meat of the piece," writes the teacher in the "project brief". "It's the analysis of the work and its relevance that make it a critical reading, rather than just a summary".[10] [Fig. 4]

The history of graphic design thus proves to be an echo chamber for fundamental social and political issues that are still highly topical today, particularly those concerning the dynamics of dominance and emancipation. The history of advertising, for instance, is closely linked to that of capitalism, sexism and colonial violence—to which advertising not only bears witness, but also serves as an instrument. But graphic design history also records the memory of past militant and protest movements, which still inform certain contemporary positions. Its teaching provides a forum for discussion of these social and ideological phenomena. In the words of Gui Bonsiepe, a former teacher at the Hochschule für Gestaltung in Ulm, Germany:

Even if one dismisses the modernist project, its programmatic stance *vis-à-vis* the future remains valid, and the disposition to consider how to change existing social relations remains not only desirable, but necessary. In such a context, history reveals its relevance when understood not chronologically, as a sequence of threaded facts, but as an

10 "People's Graphic Design Archives x Instagram Histories" [https://teachingresource.aiga.org/project/pgda-x-instagram-histories/]

[Fig. 3] David Reinfurt, A *New* Program for Graphic Design, 2020

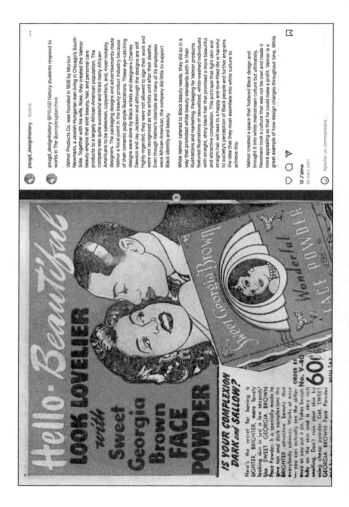

explanation of the past—and of the present through the past. (Bonsiepe, 2022, p. 270)

Among other things, students are always curious about how their profession came to be organized the way it is: namely, split (in Europe, at least) between cultural commissioning on the one hand and advertising on the other. Putting the rejection of advertising into historical perspective (from the glorification of modern advertising in the early 20th century to its denigration by left-wing intellectuals in the 1960s) brings up some fundamental ethical issues, and questions the role of graphic design in the social order—a debate more pressing than ever nowadays as crises of all kinds are coming to a head. Retracing the history of advertising also provides an opportunity to explore visual material that has been largely overlooked by "canonical" history: a very photographic style of graphic design with highly repetitious layouts, in which the creativity often lies in the copy and slogans produced by copywriters and editors rather than in the layout. Confronting 1950s and '60s ads—and the stereotypes (especially gender stereotypes) they convey—from a present-day perspective provides exercise in critical skills that are not only useful, but also necessary.

[Fig. 4] Instagram post by Portland State University student Kelsey Zuberbuehler for the "People's Graphic Design Archive x Instagram Histories" project, 2021

Which history?

2

At art schools, courses on graphic design history are integrated into a body of theoretical teaching, whose format and accreditation methods are often close to those of university courses. Students engage in reading, documentary research, critical discussion and various forms of writing (descriptions, summaries, analyses). Working on these academic skills may sometimes seem intimidating or laborious to students, who often need to be reminded that they're not all that academic or remote from the skills developed in workshop courses. Many projects require documentary research, for example, which often serves as a springboard for design projects. What's more, practical training at art schools involves a great deal of critical activity—specifically, the ability to understand and discuss one's own and others' work. Students enroll in these courses to get critical feedback from teachers and peers during discussion sessions about the choices they've made and the reasoning behind those choices, how the work "holds together" and how it might gain in substance or depth. These critiquing sessions draw on skills that are also developed in academic courses, such as the ability to formulate pertinent questions, argue a point, allow for complexity, express subtleties and nuances, and get beyond mere subjective opinion. These skills can also be freely applied to the work of one's predecessors, which is bound to have beneficial effects on all sorts of skills that are fundamentally linked to design.

Beyond "design thinking"

In joining the field of design and its methodologies, the "graphic arts", which have become "graphic design", have inherited a system of thought that views creation through the prism of a particular methodology. "Design thinking" is often simplistically presented as a process that leads from the identification of a problem to its resolution in the production of forms or objects, via more or less predetermined stages, including the identification of projects similar in theme, method or medium. While we can imagine that a few contemporaries' work might have some relevance in this system, what about historical "references"? What's the use of knowing that the scroll function in web design actually refers to the earliest form of the book (papyrus rolls called *volumen*) or that advertising logotypes are descendants of heraldry? Does reviewing Gerd Arntz's pictograms for the International System of Typographic Picture Education (Isotype) help in designing the interface for a smartphone application in the present day and age?

Actually, it may be assumed that studying history affects students in a far more subconscious way than in the form of the "reference" cited, and, in particular, through the observation and understanding of forms or ways of resolving technical and communication problems, which can be updated for and in the present. This is the argument of British graphic designer and historian Richard Hollis:

> If you learn from what people have done very well previously and try to reconstruct what was happening, both in their minds and at the time, and what technology was available, it helps you to understand the process of design. Even if it doesn't seem directly relevant to you as you sit in front of a computer screen, it builds an understanding of how things are produced and consumed visually. (Hollis, 2020, p. 191)

An intimately appropriated history is more useful to a designer than mere book knowledge. It may even take the form of a *kinesic* experience. In his practical workshops, for example, typographer François Chastanet has students work on the manual gesture of the *ductus,* the physical strokes involved in creating letterforms, in particular through the practice of *Dishu,* a technique in Chinese calligraphy that involves writing with water on the ground in public spaces.[Fig. 5] Well aware of the attendant anachronism (who still writes by hand in our day?), Chastanet explains that the exercise is nevertheless fundamental to understanding the skeletons of the Roman alphabet:

> The main challenge is our knowledge of the origins of the letters mainly used today on-screen, and sometimes reproduced and printed.[...] Re-living the calligraphic experience of historical canons represents a special entry point for the aspiring type designer, so as to develop his ability to see and grasp forms. [...] This phase involving the rediscovery of the history of writing makes it possible to posit the obvious difference between calligraphy [...], lettering [...] and type design, which is essential for an understanding of the different issues of drawing. (Chastanet, 2018, p. 118)

Chastanet views some latter-day writing practices, in particular graffiti and certain large-format productions in public spaces, as direct heirs to this ancient handwriting gesture. Rather than trying to draw on the history of ideas, it's more important to realize the paths by which that history has informed the present-day world.

Furthermore, it's becoming increasingly clear that the rhetoric of "problem-solving" belongs to an outmoded modernist paradigm that hems design (and graphic design along with it) in a misleading representation as a linear mechanical process with guaranteed results, as well as in the misconception that problems exist independently of the people trying to solve them (Dubberly, 2022). Geoff Kaplan, a professor of graphic design at Yale, does a good job of summing up this suspicion:

> Since my undergraduate training in graphic design in the early to mid-'80s, when graphic design was only and always described as a "problem-solving" activity, I have been suspicious of this characterization. What problems? And if design is about solving problems, then why do so many persist (war, hunger, income inequality and homelessness, racism and anti-semitism...)? The problems that we graphic designers are attempting to "solve" must not be too difficult or "wicked". (Kaplan, 2022, p.24)

Unless, as suggested by his colleague Anne Burdick, "these 'problems' could be thought of and acted upon as philosophical ones as opposed to, say, mathematical; as sociological, not scientific; as historical, not purely technological" *(ibid.)*. This hypothesis calls for graphic design pedagogy to reinforce skills of observation and reflection on society, its media and signs.

Learning to see

Familiarizing oneself with graphic design history provides an opportunity to sharpen the eye and develop one's ability not only to read images (Dondis, 1973), but also to understand how images are imbued with meaning, how they manage, by visual means, to convey meanings—which can then be explained in words. The idea forged by structuralist linguistics that images are endowed with a language of their own became firmly entrenched in 1960s graphic culture. Witness the success of the term "visual communication", which was pioneered for one of the courses at the Hochschule für Gestaltung in Ulm (1953–1968). Within a matter of just a few years, it gained a popularity that the term "graphic design" would still have to wait a long time for in continental Europe. Josef Müller-Brockmann, an eminent Zurich graphic designer and leading exponent of the "Swiss style", used it for the title of his *History of Visual Communication* (1971), while in Paris the journal *Communication & Langages* published some seminal theoretical essays about posters, typography and advertising. In their wake, the term "visual communication" caught on in many art and design schools to designate standard courses of training in graphic design.[11]

Students in "visual communication" at the school in Ulm were taught mathematics, sociology and cultural history, as well as cognitive science geared towards Gestalt psychology and the theories of Gyorgy Kepes (Buckley, 2022). His modernist theories of vision are based on the idea that certain graphic forms have immutable semantic characteristics and that, if properly identified and used, they can determine the impression of balance, movement, intensity, etc., of a visual composition. This yields some practical applications for the design of visual messages, but ultimately provides relatively few tools for reading graphic productions as "semantic machines". And for good reason: Gestalt principles, based on the observation of scientific facts of human perception, pay no attention to the variety of historical contexts. What's more, they are confined to very simple images—essentially, to basic geometric shapes and combinations thereof.

Real training in interpreting images in the field of graphic design calls for other interpretive tools, in particular those used by semiology since Roland Barthes' first writings on advertising and the magazine press. Although Barthes' semiology does not pay much attention to the actual contexts

11   At the time of writing, the term is still used at the University of Applied Sciences and Arts of Western Switzerland (HES-SO).

of images,[12] it forms part of an epistemological system that compares images with one another and seeks to articulate major cross-cultural concepts ("myth"). It is actually essential to place images in the context of visual habits as well as expectations based on the type of product, service or event advertised, and their positioning in the commercial and cultural offerings of their day and age. As semiologist Pierre Fresnault-Deruelle, a savvy decipherer of illustrated posters, observes: "An image is always an image of an image. In other words, adventitious configurations 'behind' (or 'beneath') the image before our eyes come to light as if through rear projection" (Fresnault-Deruelle, 2011, p.10). We can make out "motifs" (in the sense of *leitmotifs*) recycled from one poster to another, recurring effects that allow us to go beyond the isolated instance or the semantic effects of a single given production. Hence, training the designer eye clearly depends on media research skills and, in particular, image research.

12   In his famous analysis of Panzani ads for its "deluxe Italian pasta" in "The Rhetoric of the Image" (1964), Barthes refers to it as a poster (when in fact it was an ad in the press) and says nothing about the client and its target audience, not even pointing out for example that Panzani is a French brand whose "Italianness" is therefore entirely fake.

Search methods in terrain uncharted
by Wikipedia

One assignment frequently given to students in graphic design history courses is to conduct a little documentary research on a historical graphic object. Paradoxically, the exercise proves all the more effective if the object to be commented on is wholly or almost unknown, i.e. not among the masterpieces of poster history and not duly catalogued and described by the public collections in which they are kept. But this undertaking is not wholly without risks...

First of all, there's no denying that the overwhelming majority of documentary research is now carried out online and it's becoming increasingly futile to privilege "reliable" printed sources over "unreliable" digital sources, given how porous these media have now become (printed books exist in digital or digitized versions on the Internet, and many books published nowadays draw on online sources of information) and, above all, given the wealth of collective intelligence made available on the Internet, epitomized by Wikipedia

—even if it does a very poor or imprecise job of covering graphic design history.[13] Nevertheless, online documentary research on design history has particularities of its own. First of all, as Matthew Bird, a teacher of industrial design at the Rhode Island School of Design, points out, it is dominated by images:

> The role of images in research has changed dramatically since the advent of the Internet. Historically, an image was used as an attachment, an illustration. We worked with information, and then included the image to explain or clarify. Today it is more common for an image to be the first contact point for an object. Any information, if it is lucky enough to stay attached, arrives later in the discovery process. (Bird, 2019)

As a result, documentary research on graphic design history often starts with navigating vast corpora of images, reproductions of posters, pages from newspapers, advertisements, book and album covers, etc. Images abound, but the referencing thereof is sometimes erroneous, often simply absent. Since graphic productions are rarely signed, mis-

---

13   By way of example, at the time of writing (fall of 2023), there's nothing on French Wikipedia about Nelly Rudin, a major Swiss graphic designer, and only scant biographical notes on Bauhaus typographer Herbert Bayer, Béatrice Warde, a typographer and writer on the subject of typography, the great Dutch modernist Piet Zwart or the French typographer Roger Excoffon.

attributions are legion, and all too frequently passed on and amplified by social networks like Pinterest, Redbubble and even the Google Images search engine. A poster by Ikko Tanaka, for instance, is making the rounds as the cover of a background music cassette for Muji stores.[Fig. 6][14] Student projects parodying certain graphic designers end up being referenced as works by the designers themselves. Paperback editions of books are dated on the basis of—or attributed to the publishers of—the original edition. While this is often disorientating, it turns out to be an edifying experience that heightens awareness of the need to cross-reference sources—one of the basic rules of serious research—and to use the Internet for what it is: a network of individual and institutional content providers. As Matthew Bird points out:

> Each on-line resource had advantages and disadvantages making it useful, but unreliable when used in isolation as a research tool. Using web resources as a network of cross-linked tools groups their strengths to work past individual weaknesses. They are transformed from a mere curiosity to a groundbreaking resource. (Bird, 2019)

Students often use the Internet as a vast library, the contents of which are called up by typing a few keywords into a search engine. But to document

14   Designer Robert Beatty devoted a Twitter thread to this misapprehension in 2021 [https://www.are.na/block/11200287].

a graphic object on the web, they need to explore various sites, and it's impossible to know beforehand which ones: fan blogs, reverse image search tools, second-hand bookshops specializing in old books, record stores, press archives, online selling sites and marketplaces, in an attempt to track down vanished brands, contemporary debates, poster campaigns, even some retired graphic designers only too happy to share their stories. The Internet holds the promise of a demythologizing research experience that students discover to be surprisingly unceremonious. And in the end, it's very gratifying to be able to share what are often little-known results.

3

Reflecting on how the graphic design community conceives of history, what it does with it and how, historian Catherine de Smet refers to "regimes of historicity", a term coined by François Hartog to describe the way in which social groups make use of a shared experience of time. Graphic design has a particular relationship to time, its own special "regime of historicity". "Time is undoubtedly experienced in a particular way in graphic design, between the long duration of writing, the relative stability of letterforms and the short life of plenty of printed productions, aside from books," writes Catherine de Smet (2017).

At art schools, it is important to consider these "experiences of time" as fundamental components of creation. Like all design disciplines, graphic design is an activity constituted and informed by anticipation. It involves foreseeing everything from the work in the studio and physical production to the printing press, announcing events that have yet to materialize, anticipating the public's reaction, designing objects that will endure for centuries (e.g. books) or change within a few years (visual identities). Graphic design students must project into the future, which will also form the backdrop to their professional future, so it is well worth their while for them to think about what holds together the past, the present and the future.

The didactic benefit of a widely used graphic form naturally comes to mind in this connection: the timeline. One of the oldest ways of visually presenting chronological information, it has the drawback of representing mathematical, linear, homogeneous time, which is ultimately very different from individual human perception of the passage of time, which is made up of discontinuities, subdivisions and highly variable impressions of time (Drucker, 2014, p.75). Bringing these representations into line is a delicate task, but a real job for a designer, one that also enables us to situate ourselves personally and intimately on the timeline of history.

One outstanding example that hasn't lost any of its vivacity over the years dates from 1961, when Polish artist Stefan Themerson was invited to give a lecture on Kurt Schwitters at Cambridge. The audience was made up of students in their early twenties, who struck Themerson as being quite detached from the avant-garde issues that

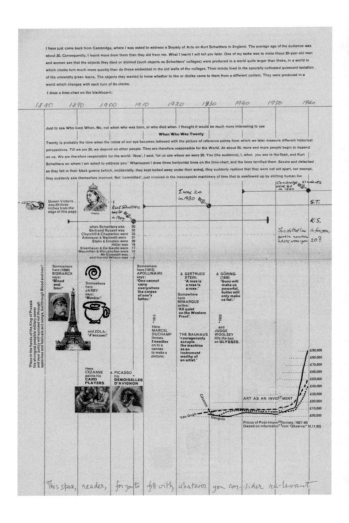

once drove Schwitters. By drawing a timeline on the blackboard (which was later reproduced in the British magazine *Typographica*), he helped them understand what the world was like fifty years earlier, when Schwitters was twenty, and how he might well have viewed the major events of his day. The timeline included a number of key dates in the history of Great Britain and modern art, but above it he drew parallel timelines representing the lives of the students and himself, showing where each was at the age of twenty relative to the timeline of history. "They suddenly realized that they were not set apart, not exempt, they suddenly saw themselves involved. Not 'committed', just involved in the inescapable machinery of time that is always swallowed up by shifting human lives" (Themerson, 1964). As the lecture went on, Themerson added more and more personal notes, subjective comments and various interconnections between the timelines, thereby illustrating the Dadaist spirit and the annotative zeal typical of Schwitters' work in Britain (1940–1948) at the end of his life.[Fig. 7]

This sort of ramifying representation eludes the linearity and teleology traditionally associated with a timeline. In this manner, critical history has encouraged historiographical practices that don't seek to describe major movements or changing trends, but proceed instead by little leaps and setbacks. Some teachers argue that graphic design history should not be taught chronologically anymore, that the curriculum should revolve around "issues" (e.g. typography, information design, cultural appropriation, stereotypes, universal design, ethics) so as to present students more directly with the cyclical nature of that history, rather than with grand, overarching narratives (Griffin, 2019).

Graphic design students are particularly receptive to accounts of the historical configurations in which their predecessors imagined or projected the future of their profession. What prospects were they anxious or enthusiastic about? What did they foresee about where we are today? What "crises" did they overcome? There are plenty of examples of both enthusiastic and pessimistic predictions. Since the late 19th century, for instance, there has been no end of prophecies of the demise of the printed book, which was purportedly doomed to be replaced in time by other media, whether electric or audio (Ludovico, 2012). Far from deploring this eventuality, avant-garde artists and typographers as early as the 1920s and '30s looked forward to the acceleration of communication, the ascendancy of photography and motion pictures and electrical signals, and they recognized and seized the opportunity to reinvent traditional editorial forms: "cinematographic" books or books designed to be read aloud (e.g. Lissitzky's above-mentioned *For the Voice*).

But past changes in graphic technologies and their impact on the profession have the most striking potential for identification in the present-day context. Ever since the industrialization of the profession in the 19th century, graphic designers have constantly felt they are "in crisis", especially in publishing and the press, which have been most markedly impacted by technological innovations that have increased productivity—sometimes at the expense of quality and jobs. The same anxiety about the threat of innovations was expressed by engraving artists faced with competition from photoengraving techniques, by Linotype operators supplanted by typists at phototypesetting shops—who were replaced in turn a decade later by desktop publishing. By making these printing and publishing tools available to everyone, desktop publishing was regarded as the greatest threat ever to the profession. And yet, some forty years on, there are more professional graphic designers than ever before. In the current context of the development of artificial intelligence and the not-so-distant prospect of automating many layout and content production tasks, seeing and hearing these 20th-century predecessors confronted with the same fears of being replaced by blind machines actually gives cause for optimism about the profession's ability to reinvent itself, whilst remaining lucid about the aesthetic, ideological and social changes brought about and accompanied by technological developments.

Courses in graphic design history, as in the history of art, architecture and object design, often involve the use of reproductions: photos projected onto a big screen in the classroom or reproduced on the pages of textbooks, or scrolling through digital resources and databases. But it's hard to make out the actual size and volume of the items shown in these reproductions. The result is a tendency to focus on the form of graphic productions rather than their contexts, uses and underlying ideas (Wilkins, 1992; Sfligiotti, 2022). Furthermore, in an age in which students and teachers alike comb through hundreds of pictures day in, day out, the use of reproductions is more than likely to dull the experience of aesthetic defamiliarization to which history invites us.

How can we break out of this visual anesthesia? By confronting graphic objects "in the flesh", in particular by visiting local public collections of graphic arts. The resources to be found in museums (which seldom collect posters, let alone graphic art objects in general) are rarely as rich as those of libraries with collections of printed works, which, besides posters, often cover several centuries of publishing and sometimes hold excellent themed or monographic collections. Pedagogical partnerships between art schools and collections sometimes give rise to exhibitions and/or small publications that may raise questions about the future museumization of graphic objects and the conditions in which they are conserved.[15] The following are just two examples of the emotion elicited by first-hand encounters with graphic objects.

In 2018 and 2019, Master's students from the Graphic Communication workshop at Strasbourg's Haute École des Arts du Rhin (HEAR) worked at the city's Bibliothèque des Musées de Strasbourg on a collection of Dadaist books and documents. Under the supervision of two teachers, Yohanna My Nguyen and Jérôme Saint-Loubert Bié, they put together a booklet that was then distributed at an exhibition held from April 30 to June 29, 2019. It is a small stapled notebook in a dust jacket containing four-color reproductions of detail views of the Dada publications studied by the students as well as brief essays by the students themselves describing certain aspects of Dadaist graphic design. In their presentation of this publication project, Nguyen and Saint-Loubert Bié point out this effect of visual anesthesia caused by reproductions

---

15 *Collectionner, conserver, exposer le graphisme. Entretiens autour du travail de Dieter Roth conservé au Frac Bretagne*, EEASAB-Frac Bretagne, 2015. A project carried out by students at the EESAB in Rennes under the direction of Catherine de Smet, Kévin Donnot and Isabelle Jégo.

of Dada magazines and pamphlets *ad nauseam,* "objects already overworked, often cited, analyzed, reproduced even on postcards and the covers of address books". When they "really discovered" them during their first visit to the Bibliothèque des Musées de Strasbourg with the head of the library, Franck Knoery, they were struck by what the reproductions couldn't show: their tangible side.

> The physical reality of the artifacts and the questions to which that gave rise gradually enriched our discussions. By dint of observing, handling and appreciating the details, our interest turned to the various physical characteristics of the documents, most of which we knew only from reproductions we'd seen in books and, more probably, online. How had they been produced under the constraints of that era (paper manufacture, printing and binding methods, the "physically" limited availability of wooden or lead type sets)?[16]

This experience determined the form of the publication, which brings out the "action of time", showing them "differently from the reproduction bank, frontally, with uniform lighting" so as to render their "graphic physicality through a more 'subjective' photographic approach comprising

16   Yohanna My Nguyen and Jérôme Saint-Loubert Bié, "Dada: vu et revu", DADA COLLECTION, Bibliothèque des Musées de Strasbourg–HEAR, 2019, p. 43–46. The participating students were Valentin Meynadier, Laurine Pasco and Lucile Weber.

detail and oblique views, surfaces of pages, yellowed or torn corners, rust stains, staples, archival stamps, etc."[Fig. 8] This kind of representation showing the physical form of books and other printed objects is not unprecedented in contemporary publication design, but in this particular pedagogical context it testifies to a highly embodied rapport between these aspiring graphic designers, i.e. future practitioners of print, and the history of books and publishing.

While it can sometimes prove difficult to leave the walls of the classroom, graphic objects are quite adept at penetrating those walls—an advantage not always shared by works discussed in class in other disciplines at art schools. This is particularly true of 20th-century books and magazines, which are an inexhaustible resource, easily and inexpensively to be had at second-hand booksellers' and flea markets if one is prepared to take an interest in paperbacks, mainstream magazines and their advertisements. This subject matter allows us to stray from the beaten path of the canonical narrative to turn our attention to less highbrow objects. This was the object of a pedagogical project conducted in 2018 at the Bern University of the Arts by Sarah Zeller, Sandra Bischler and Robert Lzicar with undergraduate students in the Visual Communication Department in a seminar on the history of graphic design. Against the backdrop of a large-scale research project called "Swiss Graphic Design History Revisited", led by Davide Fornari and Robert Lzicar and funded by the Swiss National Science Foundation, the teachers and students

explored graphic material that has been over-shadowed by the masterpieces of "Swiss style" that are so often exhibited and reproduced: "Anonymous everyday graphic design of past decades tells relevant stories and, at the same time, [serves] to complement well-known historical narratives with alternative and personal approaches."[17]

Using graphic objects "found in one's own home, in one's grandparents' basement or at the thrift store" and brought to class, students had to carry out documentary research and write brief personal essays about why they were interested in the form of these particular objects or about their historical significance. Their fascination with everyday amateur graphic design gave rise to discussions about historiographical processes of selection, the construction of national identity, the social significance of graphic design and the possibility of appropriating this history in the present, as indicated by the seminar's title and the ensuing exhibition: "My Own Private Swiss Graphic Design History".[Fig. 9] As in the Strasbourg project, however, this pedagogical experiment hinged on close contact with the material objects themselves, though this time around without the quasi-religious veneration associated with consulting a public collection. These postcards, beer mats, cardboard or tin packaging, magazines and banknotes were culled from real life and could be physically handled, so studying them

17   Sarah Zeller, Sandra Bischler and Robert Lzicar, course presentation [https://sgdtr.ch/fr/journal/]. The project culminated in an exhibition presented in Bern and London in the summer of 2018.

[Fig. 9] *My Own Private Swiss Graphic Design History*, HKB students' exhibition at Ambit Exhibition Space, London, July 5–27, 2018

Why History Matters to Graphic Design

was a not-so-unexpected extension of their "social life as things" (Appadurai, 2020 [1986]).

What students experienced in these workshops was "age value", a concept theorized at the very beginning of the 20th century by Alois Riegl in *The Modern Cult of Monuments*. According to Riegl, the taste for the new forms of modernity has as its corollary an attraction to the physical marks of the passage of time; satisfaction with the "wholeness" of new human productions goes hand in hand with an expectation of the dissolution of this wholeness. Consequently, when contemplating old architecture, we are aesthetically moved by the signs of nature (weathering, vegetation) and do not appreciate conspicuously new renovations. "The fundamental aesthetic principle of our time," according to the Viennese philosopher, lies in "the perception of the necessary cycle of genesis and disappearance" (Riegl, 2013 [1903], p.77). "Historical knowledge thus also becomes a source of the aesthetic pleasure elicited by age." (*ibid.*, p.83). The philosophical paradigm of this theory is obviously Western—other cultural realms, as we know, show no such concern for old things—and freighted with the moral weight of vanity *(memento mori)*, but Riegl's thesis enables us to name and theorize the emotion felt not only in contemplating architecture, but also in the presence of any "thing" from the past. In particular, it is undeniably felt in the presence of graphic objects that record the passing of fashions. This emotion develops in students a capacity for a form of aesthetic decentering that is essential to their future vocation.

> Training is concerned with preparing the student for specific tasks: the known. But education concerns itself with preparing for the future: the unknown. (Thomas Ockerse, 2022, p.136)

In recent years, art school students and teachers have had the impression that they're heading into the unknown. What will professional graphic design involve in the future? Under what social, economic, climatic and technological conditions will we produce images and messages, and for whom? One thing's for sure: the next generation of graphic designers will have to be even more adaptable than their predecessors. How can we prepare them for this if not by getting them to feel curious about difference and otherness, by putting them through the ordeal of incomprehension and perplexity aroused by graphic forms of the past? Contact with those forms leads to the invention of new ways of communicating, i.e. of doing graphic design, for it is up to graphic designers to create connections between people and things. Siding with history means fighting against amnesia and presentism, so it's a far more subversive choice than it would seem.

Above and beyond training graphic designers in technical skills, project methods and academic skills (reading, writing, research), the affective and emotional benefits of exploring graphic design history need to be recognized and defended. Discovering real printed objects whose paper has turned yellow over time and feeling moved by traces of the work and efforts of their predecessors is an experience that can only be fully appreciated with a certain poetic spirit. The history of graphic design cannot be practiced with a dry eye and a cold heart. It calls for a tender curiosity about the ways and everyday lives of yesteryear, as well as an effort of imagination to transport us to ages before our time: an aesthetic pleasure that is far from being superficial or at least merits consideration as a mode of appropriation we can encourage in students.

Bibliography

Appadurai, Arjun (ed.), *The Social Life of Things,* Cambridge University Press, 1986

Bird, Matthew, "Using Digital Tools to Work Around the Canon", in Jennifer Kauffman-Buhler, Victoria Rose Pass and Christopher S. Wilson (eds.), *Design History Beyond the Canon,* London, New York: Bloomsbury Visual Arts, 2019, 111–125

Bonsiepe, Gui, "On the Heteronomy of Design in a Post-Utopian Age", in Geoff Kaplan (ed.), *After the Bauhaus, Before the Internet: A History of Graphic Design Pedagogy,* New York, San Francisco: no place press, 2022, 264–270

Buckley, Craig, "The Crux of Coordination: Visual Communication at the Hochschule für Gestaltung, Ulm", in Geoff Kaplan (ed.), *After the Bauhaus, Before the Internet: A History of Graphic Design Pedagogy,* New York, San Francisco: no place press, 2022, 96–120

Chastanet, François, "Pour un ductus urbain", in *Lettres de Toulouse.* Expérimentations pédagogiques dans le dessin de lettres, Montreuil: B42, 2018, 117–123

De Smet, Catherine and De Bondt, Sarah, *Graphic Design. History in the Writing (1983–2011),* London: Occasional Papers, 2012

De Smet, Catherine, "Régimes d'historicité", in *Les Formes de l'histoire,* Paris: B42–CNAP, 2017, 147–161

Dondis, Donis A., *A Primer of Visual Literacy,* Cambridge (Mass.): MIT Press, 1973

Drucker, Johanna and McVarish, Emily, *Graphic Design History: A Critical Guide,* Boston: Pearson, 2009

Drucker, Johanna, *Graphesis: Visual Forms of Knowledge Production,* Cambridge (Mass.): Harvard University Press, 2024

Dubberly, Hugh, "Why We Should Stop Describing Design as 'Problem-Solving'", in Geoff Kaplan (ed.), *After the Bauhaus, Before the Internet: A History of Graphic Design Pedagogy,* New York, San Francisco: no place press, 2022, 274–287

EnsadLab Type: Baldinger, André and Millot, Philippe, "Création de caractères typographiques : entre histoire et novation", in *Design graphique. Les Formes de l'histoire,* Paris, Montreuil: CNAP–B42, 2017

Fornari, Davide and Lzicar, Robert (eds.), *Mapping Graphic Design History in Switzerland Is Not Just Another Book that Retells the Success Story of Swiss Graphic Design,* Zurich: Triest, 2016

Fornari, Davide and Lzicar, Robert (eds.). *Swiss Graphic Design Histories,* Zurich: Scheidegger & Spiess, 2021

Foster, Hal, "An Archival Impulse", *October,* No. 110, October 2004, 3–22

Fresnault-Deruelle, Pierre, *L'intelligence des affiches,* Paris: Pyramid, 2011

Friend, Leon, *Graphic Design: A Library of Old and New Masters in the Graphic Arts,* New York, London: Whittlesey House, McGraw-Hill, 1936

Godard, Keith, "Pioneering Graphic Design History", in Steven Heller (ed.), *Teaching Graphic Design History,* New York: Allworth Press, 2019, 23–30

Griffin, Dori, "Teaching Graphic Design History," February 22, 2019, https://arthistoryteachingresources.org/2019/02/teaching-graphic-design-history/

Heller, Steven and Chwast, Seymour, *Graphic Style: From Victorian to Post-Modern,* London: Thames and Hudson, 1988

Heller, Steven (ed.), *The Education of a Graphic Designer,* New York: Allworth Press, 1998

Heller, Steven and Ballance, Georgette (eds.), *Graphic Design History,* New York: Allworth Press, 2001

Heller, Steven, *Teaching Graphic Design History,* New York: Allworth Press, 2019

Hodik Barbara, and Remington, Roger (eds.), *The First Symposium on the History of Graphic Design: Coming of Age: April 20–21, 1983,* New York: Rochester Institute of Technology, 1984

Hollis, Richard, "It's Rather an Attitude: Richard Hollis, interviewed by Brad Haylock", in Luke Wood and Brad Haylock (eds.), *One and Many Mirrors: Perspectives on Graphic Design Education,* London: Occasional Papers, 2020, 180–193

Jobling, Peter and Crowley, David, *Graphic Design: Reproduction and Representation Since 1800,* Manchester, New York: Manchester University Press, 1996

Kaplan, Geoff (ed.), *After the Bauhaus, Before the Internet: A History of Graphic Design Pedagogy,* New York, San Francisco: no place press, 2022

Kneller, G. F., *The Art and Science of Creativity,* London: Holt, Rinehart and Winston, 1965

Ludovico, Alessandro, *Post-Digital Print: The Mutation of Publishing Since 1894,* Paris: B42, 2012

Meggs, Philip B., *A History of Graphic Design,* London: Allen Lane, 1983

Müller-Brockmann, Josef, *A History of Visual Communication,* Teufen: Niggli, 1971

Nova, Nicolas, *Enquête/ Création en design,* Geneva: HEAD–Publishing, 2021

Ockerse, Thomas, "Toward Design as a Reflective Practice", in Geoff Kaplan (ed.), *After the Bauhaus, Before the Internet: A History of Graphic Design Pedagogy,* New York, San Francisco: no place press, 2022, 127–148

Poynor, Rick, *Transgression. Graphisme et postmodernisme,* Paris: Pyramid, 2003

Poynor, Rick, "Out of the Studio: Graphic Design History and Visual Studies," *Design Observer,* Jan. 1, 2011, www.designobserver.com/ feature/out-of-the-studio-graphic-design-history-and-visual-studies/24048

Rand, Paul, "Confusion and Chaos. The Seduction of Contemporary Graphic Design", *AIGA Journal of Graphic Design,* Vol. 10, No. 1, 1992, www.paulrand.design/writing/ articles/1992-confusion-and-chaos-the-seduction-of-contemporary-graphic-design.html

Reinfurt, David, *A *New* Program for Graphic Design,* Los Angeles: Inventory Press, New York: D.A.P. 2020

Riegl, Alois, *Le Culte Moderne des monuments,* French translation by Jacques Boulet (ed. orig. *Der Moderne Denkmalkultus,* Vienna: Braumüller, 1903), Paris: L'Harmattan, 2013

Scotford, Martha, "Verbal and Visual Translation of Mayakovsky's and Lissitsky's 'For Reading Out Loud'", *Visible Language,* Vol. 22, No. 2–3, Spring 1988, 195–222

Scotford, Martha, "Is There A Canon of Graphic Design History?", *AIGA Journal of Design,* Vol. 9, No. 2, 1991, 37–44

Sfligiotti, Silvia, "Out of Scale, Out of Context. The Use of Images in the Teaching of Graphic Design History", *Medium,* January 5, 2022, https://silviasfligiotti.medium.com/out-of-scale-out-of-context-the-use-of-images-in-the-teaching-of-graphic-design-history-33f958c9c0b7

Shehab, Bahia and Nawar, Haytham, *A History of Arab Graphic Design,* Cairo: American University of Cairo Press, 2020

Sunier, Coline and Mazé, Charles, *Dossier Fernand Baudin,* Dijon: Les Presses du réel, 2013

Themerson, Stefan, "Kurt Schwitters on a Time-Chart", *Typographica,* No. 16, 1967, np.

Vandenbunder, Jérémie, "Savoirs théoriques et production de discours dans les écoles supérieures d'art", *Marges,* No. 22, 2016, 87–98

Wilkins, Bridget, "No More Heroes: Why is Design so Obsessed with Appearance?", *Eye Magazine,* Vol. 6, No. 2, 1992, 4–7

Wood, Luke and Haylock, Brad (eds.), *One and Many Mirrors: Perspectives on Graphic Design Education,* London: Occasional Papers, 2020

Image credits

Clémence Imbert is a teacher and historian of graphic design. Her research to date has focused on the history of graphic design exhibitions for her PhD at Paris 8 in 2017 and on the history of book covers (*Les Couvertures de livres. Une histoire graphique,* Actes Sud—Imprimerie Nationale, 2022, Prix d'Académie 2023). She is a lecturer in the Visual Communication Department at the Geneva University of Art and Design (HEAD–Genève, HES-SO).

HEAD–Publishing, 2024

Title: Why History Matters
to Graphic Design

Original title:
Ce que l'histoire fait
au graphisme

Author: Clémence Imbert

Manifestes collection edited
by Julie Enckell Julliard and
Anthony Masure

Editorial coordinator:
Faye Corthésy

Translator: Eric Rosencrantz

Proofreader: Christopher Scala

Graphic charter:
Dimitri Broquard

Graphic design:
Alicia Dubuis

Shape of the M on the book
cover: Sara Gamito Galhano
and Claudia Dussex

Fonts:
ABC Whyte (Dinamo, 2019),
Lyon Text (Commercial Type,
2009)

Printed by Imprimerie Prestige
Graphique, Plan-les-Ouates

ISBN : 978-2-940510-87-0

Legal deposit: September 2024